South American Myths & Legends

As told by Philip Ardagh

Illustrated by Syrah Arnold

Myth or Legend?	2
The Myths and Legends of South America	4
How the Stars Came	7
Fire and the Jaguar	13
A World of Endless Skies	19
Earth, Fire, and Flood	25
The Inca—Chosen People of the Sun	31
The Voyage of the Poppykettle	37
Asare and the Alligators	43
Index	48

Dillon Press
New York

MYTH OR LEGEND?

Long before people could read or write, stories were passed on by word of mouth. Every time they were told, they changed a little, with a new character added here and a twist to the plot there. From these ever-changing tales, myths and legends were born.

WHAT IS A MYTH?

A myth is a traditional story that isn't based on something that really happened and is usually about superhuman beings. Myths are made up, but they often help to explain local customs or natural phenomena.

WHAT IS A LEGEND?

A legend is very much like a myth. The difference is that a legend might be based on an event that really happened, or a person who really existed. That's not to say that the story hasn't changed over the years.

THE SOUTH AMERICAN CONTINENT

South America is the fourth biggest continent in the world. It makes up about 12 percent of the earth's land. For a continent so vast, its population is quite small, with only about 5.6 percent of the world's people. The biggest country in South America is Brazil. Other countries include Chile, Peru, and Colombia. Today most South Americans live in big cities, but the myths and legends in this book come from the peoples of the continent's mountains, forests, and grasslands.

CONTRASTING CLIMATES

Forty percent of South America is tropical, with high temperatures and a humid climate. Parts of Peru and Chile, however, are among the driest places on the planet.

DIFFERENT PEOPLES, DIFFERENT MYTHS

The European conquest of South America began in the 16th century. Because of this European influence, most modern South Americans live in towns and cities and are Christians. Before the conquest the Inca people were probably the most powerful South Americans. Many other small groups were scattered across the continent—each with its own myths and legends.

HOW DO WE KNOW?

There are still some South Americans, especially the peoples of the rain forest, who practice their old beliefs. It is important to remember that what are seen by some people as myths and legends are seen by others as their religion. Many of these myths and legends were recorded by the conquering Europeans.

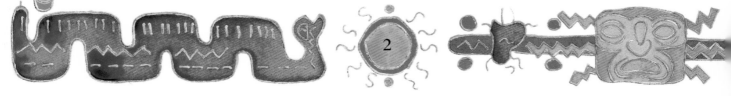

The myths and legends in this book were told by different South American peoples. This map shows where these peoples lived. The Inca Empire, whose boundaries are shown with a red line, grew up over time. Here it is shown at the height of its power (1438–1525).

KAYAPÓ

SHERENTE

CARAJÁ

BORORO

INCA EMPIRE

TUPINAMBA

This map also shows the variety of landscapes found in South America. Much more of the continent used to be rain forest —a source of food and shelter for both people and animals.

Mountains
Deserts
Rain forest
Grasslands

NOTE FROM THE AUTHOR
Myths and legends from different cultures were told in different ways. The purpose of this book is to tell new versions of these old stories, not to try to copy the way in which they were first told. I hope that you enjoy them and that this book will make you want to find out more about the South Americans and their myths and legends.

THE MYTHS & LEGENDS OF SOUTH AMERICA

The different native peoples of South America—sometimes called South American Indians—have a huge number of different myths and legends, told in hundreds of different languages. Many of these stories have common themes.

SHARED BELIEFS

Ancient South American civilizations had a similar approach to the way they saw the world around them. Mountains, rivers, plants, and animals were all seen as having supernatural and magical significance. Although there were some differences between peoples, myths and legends often had common themes.

SHARED MYTHS

One myth, shared by many groups, is that all food grew from one tree. When the tree was cut down, all the different fruits fell from its branches, and all the waters of the world sprang from its trunk.

THE INCA EMPIRE

The Inca were a people who built an empire along the Andes Mountains down the west coast of South America. Their empire stretched from present-day Ecuador, and included parts of present-day Peru, Bolivia, Chile, and Argentina.

THE CONQUERING INCA

The Inca took many of the myths and legends of the South American groups they conquered and shaped them to fit their own beliefs.

THE POWER OF POTTERY

Early peoples, dating back to 800 B.C., used pottery, textiles, gold, and silver to express their mythic beliefs. They produced paintings, patterns, and carvings to show events and characters from their myths and legends.

MIXED MYTHS

Animals also play an important role in South American myths and legends. Myths about trickster turtles are an example of how myths from different parts of the world have become mixed up. Some experts think these myths were based on tales brought to South America by African American slaves, who were forced to work for white Europeans in South America and the Caribbean.

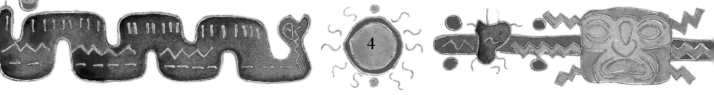

THE IMPORTANCE OF GOLD

Gold was seen as sacred by many South American peoples, including the Inca, because they linked the gleaming brightness of gold to the brilliant rays of the sun. The conquering Spaniards had a different reason for wanting gold —greed. They plundered as much Inca and South American gold as they could.

EL DORADO

El Dorado—the Golden Man—is an example of how belief in a legend can lead to death and destruction. The Spanish conquerors heard a legend about a South American ruler who was covered in gold each morning and washed it off in a lake at night. This lake was said to be thick with gold. The legend also claimed that offerings to the gods of golden trinkets were thrown into the lake.

FAILED EXPEDITIONS

European expeditions went in search of the legendary riches of El Dorado. They all failed. Many people died along the way, including many South Americans who were killed by the invaders. Sir Walter Raleigh led an English expedition which failed to find the treasure. This failure was one of the reaons why King James I had him beheaded.

This ancient South American mask of finely beaten gold represents the sun and its rays. The Inca, and those before them, worshiped sun gods.

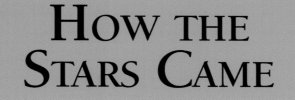

HOW THE STARS CAME

There are many South American myths about how the stars came to fill the skies. This myth, told by the Bororo people, begins with an ordinary morning in a village.

The men of the village were hunting, so the women collected their baskets and went to gather corn to make pancakes. But they found very few cobs of corn.

"This is a very poor crop," said one woman. "I've been searching all morning, and my basket is almost empty. We must find more cobs, or our men will go hungry."

"Let's ask the little one," suggested an old woman. "He's good at finding corncobs. . . . I don't know how he does it. He's so small, and the corn is so tall, but still he manages to find cobs!"

So one of the women went back to the village to find the little boy. She found him with his grandmother, who was trying to teach her pet macaw new words. Macaws are clever birds and can learn to say all kinds of things.

"Can the little one come with us and help us to find corncobs?" the woman asked the boy's grandmother.

"Of course," replied the grandmother. "Off you go, little one."

The little one returned to the cornfield with the woman.

"See what you can find," she urged him.

Sure enough, just as the old woman had predicted, the boy found corncob after corncob after corncob until all the women's baskets were full.

The women sat down in a clearing to strip the sweet corn from the cobs. Then they found flat stones and pounded the corn to make flour.

"This will mean plenty of cakes and pancakes for our men when they return," said the old woman. "They will be pleased!"

But whenever one of the women had her back turned, the little one stole some flour for himself.

"Of course, it's not really stealing," he told himself as he hid the flour in the hollow middles of bamboo shoots. "I found most of the corncobs that this flour is made from, so most of it is rightfully mine."

Soon the little one had enough hidden away for a feast. He picked up the bamboo shoots and returned to his grandmother, who had stayed behind in the village to keep an eye on the children.

"Grandma! Grandma!" he said. "I want to have a feast with all my friends . . . and here's the flour to make the cakes. Will you cook them for me?"

He tipped the flour out of the bamboo shoots into one big pile.

His grandmother's eyes widened in surprise. "Where did you get all that corn flour from, little one?" she asked in amazement.

"Little one," cackled the macaw, mimicking her words.

"You know that I went out to collect corncobs with the women," said the boy. "I helped them find so many cobs that they have more than enough corn for the men."

"So you stole this?" demanded his grandmother.

"Oh, no," lied the boy. "They said I could take as much as I could carry."

"Carry," squawked the bird.

His grandmother frowned, and then her face broke into a smile.

"I believe you," she said and began baking cakes.

Soon the grandmother's house was full of the delicious smells of freshly cooked cakes . . . and full of children, because the little one had invited all his friends to share the feast.

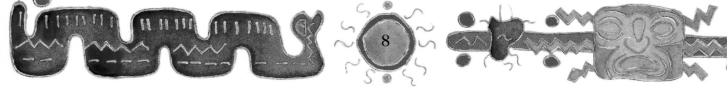

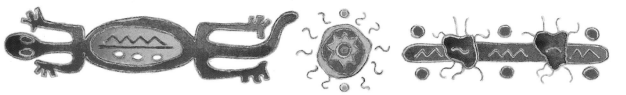

While the children ate, the boy's grandmother and her pet macaw sat in the corner and watched them fill themselves with food. She was beginning to doubt that the little one had been telling the truth. She was beginning to think that perhaps her grandson hadn't really been given the corn flour, but had stolen it.

"Is my little one a thief?" she muttered.

Her pet macaw heard the word *thief* and repeated it. "Thief!" it said, and taking a liking to the word, said it again, "Thief!"

The children fell silent.

"I don't want that silly old bird to give us away," said the little one.

"Thief!" screeched the macaw.

Without stopping to think what he was doing, the boy snatched up the bird and cut out its tongue. Some say that he then cut out his grandma's tongue to make sure that she kept quiet. But his grandma was probably frightened and upset enough not to say anything after what had happened to her poor bird.

The bad deed was done. There was no turning back. And, as so often happens, one bad thing led to another. . . . Their bellies fuller than they had been in a long time, the children swarmed out of the house after the little one and set free all the other pet macaws in the village.

Then, as slowly and as surely as the sun rises in the morning, it dawned on the little one what terrible things he had done. He had stolen the corn flour. He had cut the tongue from the bird. He had frightened his grandma. . . . Whatever next? They must flee—the children must escape before their parents found out what they'd done!

But where could they escape to where the grown-ups wouldn't find them?

"I know," said the little one. "Grown-ups aren't very good climbers because they're too heavy. Let's climb up somewhere they'll never be able to follow."

"Where?" asked a girl, with cake crumbs still around her mouth.

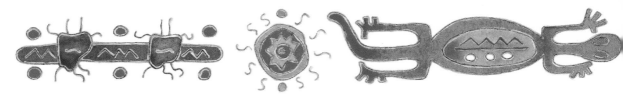

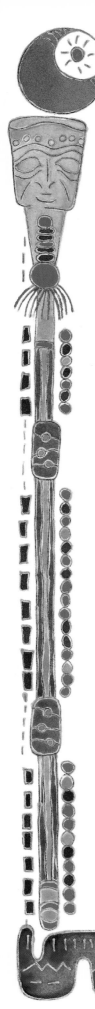

"To the sky!" cried the little one.

"But how?" asked an older boy.

"There are always ways!" said the little one, and just at that moment he spied a large creeper. It had big knots in its stem and would be easy for them to climb. Hovering by the creeper was a hummingbird.

The little one whispered something in the hummingbird's ear, and the tiny bird took one end of the creeper and flew with it up into the sky and fastened it in place.

"Hurry!" called out the little one and began to shin up the creeper. Soon a whole stream of children were climbing up into the heavens.

When the women returned to the village, their baskets filled with corn flour and ready to cook for their men, they found that their children were missing. They hurried to the house of the little one's grandmother. She was sobbing by her poor macaw.

"What's happened?" cried one woman.

"Where are all the children?" wailed another.

Then one of them caught sight of the legs of the very last child climbing up the creeper into the skies.

"Look! There they are!" she cried and raced off toward the creeper.

The other women followed, and soon they were all frantically climbing the knotted creeper to try to reach their children.

But the little one was right. This was a place where grown-ups would never be able to follow. The creeper could not take their weight and broke away from where the hummingbird had fastened it.

With a terrible "CRACK," the creeper dropped to earth like a coil of rope, and the women—the children's mothers, aunts, and cousins —fell screaming to the ground. But the earth was kind to them that day. Instead of all of the women being killed—and they surely would have been, because they fell from a great height—they were turned into different animals as they hit the dry, hard soil. This strange mixture of creatures then scampered, scurried, slithered, leapt, and ambled away.

When the men returned from the hunt that night, they expected to be greeted with the smells of cooking and the cries of children, but apart from the little one's grandmother, there was no one in sight.

"Where is everyone?" one of the hunters asked the old woman.

Tongue or no tongue, the little one's grandmother was now struck completely dumb by what she had seen. She said nothing.

A few strange animals strayed aimlessly between the houses, but the men ignored them, looking around frantically for their wives, daughters, and sons.

"What can have happened to them?" asked one of the hunters. "There is no sign of attack. . . . Magic must have been at work here."

"And what are those?" cried another in surprise, pointing up into the night sky. The men of the village gasped in amazement as they looked up at the strange lights twinkling in the blackness—the lights that we now know as stars.

With the creeper gone, the children were trapped in the heavens forever. They are still there, and they never grow old. The stars are their eyes, twinkling with tears as they weep for the terrible things they did.

FIRE AND THE JAGUAR

There are many different versions of this myth among the different groups of Kayapó people, but each one tells how people learned the secret of fire and began to cook their food.

Back in the days when people dried raw meat in the sun to make it easier to chew, a man and a boy went hunting for food. The man spotted a macaw's nest high up on a rocky ledge.

"You must climb up to the nest and see if there are any eggs in it, Botoque," he told the boy.

"Why me?" asked Botoque. "You're bigger and stronger."

"Exactly," said the man. "This is a job for someone small."

Botoque tried to climb the rock face. But there weren't any handholds or footholds. "This is hopeless!" he groaned.

"Don't be so quick to give up!" said the man, who was Botoque's sister's husband. "We must make you a ladder."

The man searched around the scrub until he spotted a fallen tree trunk. "Here," he said. "Help me drag this into the opening."

With a pair of macaws circling in the sky above them, squawking out their warning cries, Botoque and his brother-in-law began cutting footholds into the dead wood to make a ladder.

When it was finished, the man and boy dragged the tree trunk up to the rock face and leaned the ladder against it.

Botoque's eyes followed the length of the tree-trunk ladder from the very bottom right up to its tip, which only just reached the ledge where the macaws were nesting. It was a long way up.

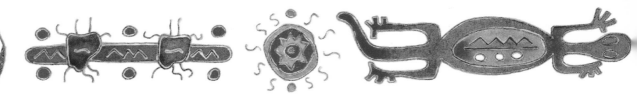

"Do you really expect me to climb that?" he asked nervously.

"Of course," said his brother-in-law. "I will hold the bottom to keep it steady."

More than a little reluctantly, Botoque climbed up and up and up until he reached the ledge. He stepped off the ladder and looked into the nest.

"How many eggs are there?" the man called up.

Botoque couldn't believe his eyes. The nest was completely empty except for two round stones.

"None!" he shouted, leaning forward to pick up the stones.

"Then what have you got in your hands?" demanded his brother-in-law, shielding his eyes against the sun to see what Botoque was doing.

"Stones!" Botoque called down. "They must have fallen off the rock face."

"You're lying!" the man shouted. "My wife's brother is a little liar! They're two lovely macaw eggs, and you want them for yourself!"

Just as Botoque put his foot back onto the tree-trunk ladder, his brother-in-law began to shake it with rage.

"Stop that!" the boy cried out in panic. "I'm not lying." He grabbed the tree trunk with both hands, and the pair of stones fell from his grasp . . . all the way down to his furious brother-in-law.

"How dare you throw stones at me!" screamed the man as one of the stones clipped him on the side of the head. He staggered backward and let go of the ladder, which fell to the ground with a mighty "CRASH." The ladder broke in two. Perhaps Botoque's brother-in-law let go on purpose. He was certainly very angry.

Fortunately for Botoque he'd had time to scramble back onto the ledge before the ladder toppled away beneath him. But unfortunately he was now trapped high up on the ledge with no way down.

"Help!" he called out. "Help me!" But his brother-in-law ignored him and walked away.

When the brother-in-law returned to the village, he told lies about Botoque, saying that he hadn't done as he was told and had run off into the undergrowth.

Botoque was alone on the narrow cliff ledge for days. The macaws were frightened by his presence and had abandoned their nest. Cold and hungry, Botoque quickly lost weight and soon was nothing more than skin and bones, his body casting a strangely shaped shadow on the dusty ground below.

Then one day a passing jaguar—a big wild cat—caught sight of the shadow and, thinking that it was some strange creature, tried to pounce on it. Every time the jaguar pounced, Botoque pulled himself back on the ledge, so his shadow disappeared from the ground.

Puzzled, the jaguar looked up and caught sight of Botoque.

"What are you?" he asked.

"I'm a human," said Botoque.

"I didn't think humans lived in nests on rocky ledges," said the jaguar, who, like all big cats, was very steady on his paws. He made his way up the rock face where no human would have found footholds.

Botoque told the jaguar about his brother-in-law's betrayal. But when the jaguar suggested he climb on his back, Botoque was nervous.

"Trust me," said the jaguar. "It is your own kind who has betrayed you, not I. Come home with me, and you can be my son."

So Botoque climbed onto the jaguar's back, and soon they reached his home. In the middle of the floor was a jatoba log, burning brightly.

"What is that?" gasped Botoque, for he had never seen anything quite so magical. The brightly colored flames seemed to dance in front of his eyes. They crackled and gave off heat, too.

"It is called fire," said the jaguar. "We cook with it."

"Cook?" asked Botoque. He had never heard this word. Humans didn't know the secret of fire, so they ate everything raw.

"You'll soon see," said the jaguar, and he called for his wife.

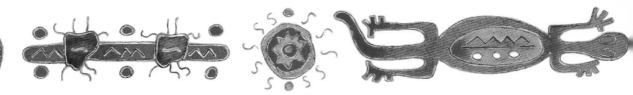

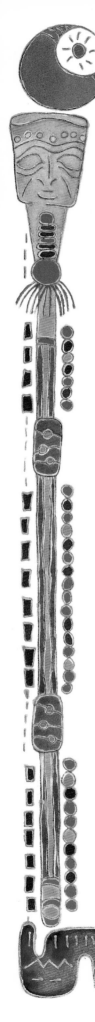

"Who is this?" asked the jaguar's wife.

"This is Botoque," said the jaguar. "He was betrayed by his own kind, so I have adopted him as our child."

"But we will soon be having a child of our own," said the jaguar's wife, who was expecting a cub. She looked at the boy by the light of the flickering flames.

"So we will have two children," said the jaguar, and that was the end of the discussion. "Now, let's eat."

And that was how Botoque became the first of his people—perhaps the first human—to eat meat cooked on a fire. It was delicious! Not only was it much easier to chew than raw meat, but the cooking brought out much more flavor. It was the best meal the boy had ever tasted. He went to sleep that night full and contented, warm in the glow of the fire.

The next morning Botoque awoke to find that the jaguar had made him a bow and arrow—a weapon no human had seen before—and the boy and animal went out hunting together. The two became very fond of each other. But the jaguar's wife was a different matter.

Whenever she and Botoque were alone together, she bared her teeth and claws. She would not let him near the meat, and sometimes he went hungry. She didn't like this new "son" in her home.

One morning, when the jaguar had gone hunting, she snarled at Botoque with such ferocity that he snatched up his bow and arrow and shot an arrow into her paw. Horrified at what he had done, Botoque felt that it was time to return to his village and to his own kind.

He grabbed a piece of cooked meat and hurried off homeward.

Back in his village there was much rejoicing from his family . . . except for his brother-in-law. Everyone had assumed Botoque was dead, yet here he was with a wondrous tale about a jaguar and something called fire. The elders tried the cooked meat and admitted that it was better than anything they'd ever tasted.

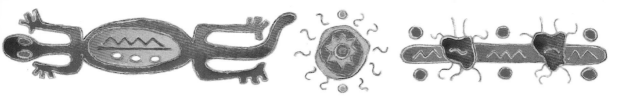

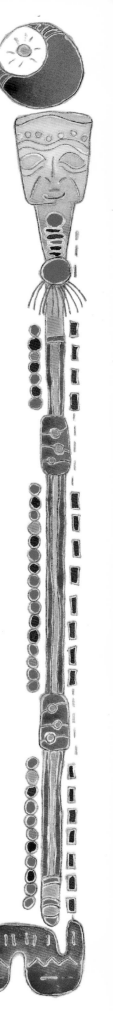

They marveled at the bow and arrow and agreed that this jaguar was, indeed, a clever fellow.

"And we must have some of this fire for ourselves," announced one of the elders. Gathering some animals around them to ask for their help, the villagers made their plans.

They crept through the forest to the jaguar's house. There a tapir heaved the burning log onto its back, and slunk back to the village with the others under the cover of darkness.

The jaguar, who had been watching them from the shadows, had a heavy heart. He had shown Botoque nothing but kindness, yet he had been betrayed. The jaguar swore never to hunt with a bow and arrow again, but to use his teeth and claws. He swore never to cook meat again, but to eat all flesh raw. The only fire he ever felt after that was a flaming rage inside him against humans—creatures who betrayed other animals as well as their own kind.

Botoque and the villagers, on the other hand, had fire to light the darkness. They could cook meat and keep warm on cold nights.

A WORLD OF ENDLESS SKIES

According to most South American myths, the first humans were immortal. They could live forever. But this Carajá myth tells a rather different story.

Long, long ago humans did not live on the surface of the earth. They lived inside it. When it was night on earth, it was daytime down below, and the reason for this was simple. When the sun set at the end of each day, it disappeared into the earth and lit this underground kingdom. Then, when it was morning, the sun rose up out of the earth and back into the sky.

Among all the people who lived in this underworld–and remember, at the beginning *all* people lived there–was one called Kaboi. Kaboi was very wise.

Sometimes he would lie on his bed at night–night down in the underworld, that is, which meant that it was daytime up on the surface–and listen to a strange cry coming from above.

Even though thick rock divided the two worlds, Kaboi could hear the cry quite clearly and wondered where it was coming from. He had no way of knowing that this was the cry of the seriema, a bird that lived on the vast grasslands of the savanna.

He had no way of knowing that the grasses themselves sang when the winds blew through them. In fact, he knew nothing of winds either, for the air in the underworld was still, and no human had ever been to the world above.

One night Kaboi could stand it no longer. He decided that he would follow the sound and try to find out where it was coming from. Several people agreed to go with him, but their names have long since been forgotten.

Kaboi and his followers climbed the rock walls of the underworld until they reached a spot where the sound was loudest.

A slight breeze blew against Kaboi's face. He had never felt a breeze before. And a new smell filled his nostrils—the smell of the grass of the savanna. Kaboi looked up, and there above him was a hole in the rock. It was a long tunnel leading to the surface.

Just then the seriema gave another cry, and the people around Kaboi cheered.

"You were right," cried one.

"You've found a way to another place!" said another with glee.

This was a very exciting moment for Kaboi. If there really was a whole new world up there, he would always be known as the one who had found the way to it.

Kaboi felt that he should say a few words to mark this important occasion, but he was too excited and hauled himself up into the entrance of the tunnel. He couldn't squeeze through the hole, though—it was very narrow, and Kaboi had a very large stomach.

"We must make the tunnel wider!" cried one.

"That won't be necessary," said Kaboi. "The most important thing is to find out what is up there," he said, pointing. "The rest of you must climb through the tunnel and explore."

They could all see how disappointed Kaboi was at not being able to visit the surface himself. But his words made sense, and the others were very eager to investigate.

Just before the last man was about to climb into the tunnel, Kaboi put his hand on his shoulder. "Don't forget to find out what makes the cry that keeps me awake at night," he said.

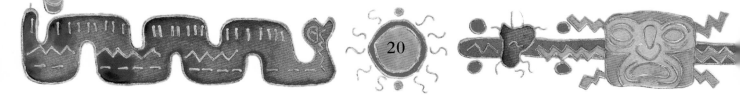

"Don't worry," said the man. "I won't."

The first people to visit the surface of the earth we now call home couldn't believe what they saw. The endless blue sky above them was like nothing they could ever have imagined. The trees, the plants, the animals, the birds. . . . Everything was so new and so exciting to their eyes.

"Kaboi has found us a paradise!" said one.

"Everyone will want to live here," said another.

"I can't wait to tell him," said another.

Someone else tried to speak, but his voice was drowned out by the cry of the seriema. "Aha!" he said in triumph when the bird had passed by. "That was the creature whose cry led us to this wondrous place. We must go back to Kaboi and report what we have found."

"We must take back things to show him, too," said the first. Everyone agreed that this was a good idea.

They gathered fruit, bees, honey, and pieces of dry wood from a dead tree; then they clambered into the tunnel to make their way back to their underground world.

"Kaboi, you have found a marvelous place," said one.

"The ceiling to the world above is not rock like the ceiling to our world, but endless blue air stretching away for as far as the eye can see," said another. He could not use the word for *sky* because no such word existed. No human had ever seen the sky–that is, until now.

Everyone started to talk at once, all eager to report the exciting things they had seen.

"Hush," said Kaboi. "There's plenty of time to discuss these things."

"Look what we brought you," said one of the search party, and they laid the fruit, bees, honey, and dry wood in front of the wise Kaboi.

Kaboi picked up a piece of fruit, smelled the skin, and bit into the flesh. Sweet juice ran down his chin. "This is delicious," he said. "It must be a wonderful world that produces such things."

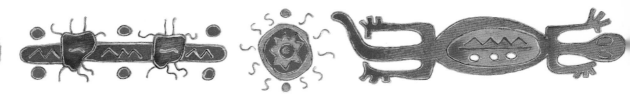

Next he studied the bees and honey.

"The insects of the upper world are hard workers," he said, then bit into a piece of honeycomb, "and the results of their labor are certainly sweet. This new world is without doubt a remarkable one —a world of plenty."

Finally he picked up a piece of dry wood. He turned it over in his hands a few times. "Where was this found?" he asked.

One of the search party pushed his way to the front.

"I found it on a tree," he said.

"And are all the trees of the upper world made of wood such as this?" asked Kaboi.

"No," said the man. "The other trees grew straight and tall, with lush green leaves. This tree was lying down and had no leaves at all—which is why I brought a piece of this wood to show you."

Kaboi looked solemn. "There is no doubt that the world up there is a beautiful world. There is no doubt that it is a fruitful world. But it is also a world where everything perishes over time."

It was clear from their faces that the people did not fully understand what the wise Kaboi was saying.

"In the world above, every living thing must one day wither away and die," he explained.

"But we die here," said the man who had brought back the pieces of dry wood.

"A very different kind of death," said Kaboi. "Here we do not shrivel or dry out like this piece of dead wood. Here we are born, and we live and go on living until, after hundreds of years, we cease to be any more," said Kaboi. "Up there, things are born, they live, and they become more and more old and withered until they perish. If any of you choose to go and live in the world above, you, too, will die long before those of us wise enough to stay."

There was a puzzled silence.

Because there was no such thing as decay for our ancestors who lived in the underground world, it was very hard for them to understand what Kaboi was saying. Even many of those who did understand decided that this was a small price to pay for living in such a beautiful new world.

And so it was that many people came to tread the path up the tunnel to live on the surface of the earth, where all of us live today —with clear skies above us and the rock beneath our feet.

We are all descended from those first people who chose this new life above ground, where death comes to us all sooner rather than later.

As for Kaboi, he remained underground, content in the knowledge that he would live a longer life than those on the surface could ever imagine.

Kaboi could still hear the cry of the seriema and could picture the bird in his mind now that it had been described to him. But he heard other cries, too—of people laughing, crying, and dying.

EARTH, FIRE, AND FLOOD

Throughout the world many myths and religious stories tell of great floods that represent a second chance for humankind. This Tupinambá myth is a story of earth, fire, and flood.

There was a time when the earth was completely flat without so much as a hill, valley, or mountain in sight. As far as the eye could see, there was just land. There were no seas or oceans, just enough lakes to provide all the water people needed to drink and all the water trees and plants needed to grow.

This world and its people were created and cared for by one called Monan. Monan existed before the beginning of time itself, so he had no beginning or end. He was, he is, and he will always be.

Monan treated humans like spoiled children and let them do whatever they liked, so long as they respected him as their creator and respected the earth he had created for them.

To begin with, this was a very satisfactory arrangement. Every day was a day of leisure and pleasure for his people, but as time went by, they became ungrateful.

"What do we need Monan for?" said one, as a fruit plopped into his mouth and he savored the sticky sweetness. "I wish he would leave us in peace."

"We have all we need," agreed another. "We certainly do not need Monan."

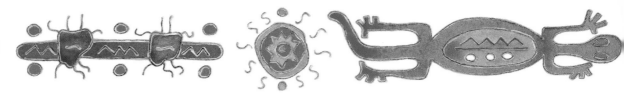

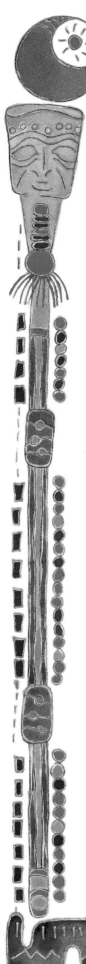

Eventually people began to speak rudely about their creator, criticizing the world he had made for them.

"I wish he'd made the days sunnier," complained one.

"I wish it weren't so bright," moaned another.

"Why is the sky such a boring blue?" said another.

Even worse, some people spoke about the earth as though it were something that had come into existence by accident. . . . They forgot about Monan altogether.

At first Monan paid no attention. He thought that his people's foolish mood would pass, and that they would soon return to being as grateful as they had been in the past. But he was wrong.

Upset at what had become of his creations, Monan turned his back on the flat earth and its inhabitants, abandoning them to life without him. But when their behavior became even more reckless, he decided that it was up to him to put right the wrong.

He sent down a terrible fire from heaven. This fire, called Tata, was so hot and so fierce that it not only destroyed every living thing, it also caused the earth to buckle and crease, which is how hills, valleys, and mountains came into being.

This would have been an end for all humans, had Monan not saved one person before sending down the fire. He couldn't bear the thought of destroying every one of his creations, so he saved a man called Irin-Mage.

Irin-Mage looked down on the burning earth and saw the flames reaching higher and higher.

"Do you want the flames to destroy the skies and stars, too?" he asked his creator. "If you do nothing to stop it, this fire of vengeance will soon reach us here in the heavens and destroy your own home!"

So Monan made it rain with a downpour the world had not seen the likes of before and has never seen since. Water poured from the skies in huge waterfalls, extinguishing the fires of Tata.

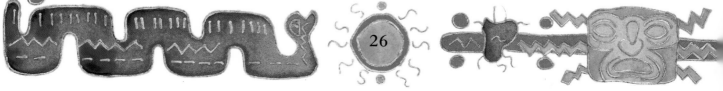

The fire's ashes were washed away, and the seas and oceans were formed. Mixed with the ashes, these waters became salty, which is why they are not like the fresh water of the rivers, lakes, and streams that were fed by later rains.

With its hills, valleys, mountains, oceans, and seas, the earth looked more beautiful than ever.

"I shall put you back there, Irin-Mage," said Monan. "The heavens are no place for you."

"I am grateful," said the only living human being. "You saved my life, and now you are returning me to a wonderful world . . . but I will be so lonely with no one to share it."

Monan looked kindly upon the man. "You are a good man," he said, "and I am glad that it was you that I chose to save. I will make you a wife so that she may share this new world with you. May you have many children together, for it is from you that all people will begin."

With that, Monan placed Irin-Mage and his new wife on earth.

Over time Irin-Mage and his wife had many children, but none were more powerful than their son Maira-Monan, named after the creator who had given humankind a second chance.

Maira-Monan was a great shaman, or medicine man, and knew all the secrets of nature. He liked to live on his own, but shared many of his secrets with others to help make life on earth easier. He taught the people the secret of fire and how to grow their own crops.

But Maira-Monan had even mightier powers than this. It was he who changed animals into all the different species we know today. When Monan placed Maira-Monan's parents on earth after the fire and flood, he gave them many different kinds of trees and plants, but all the animals were the same. It was Maira-Monan who used his skills to make them different. It was he who turned them into everything from armadillos and egrets to piranhas and vultures. He filled the land, water, and air with life.

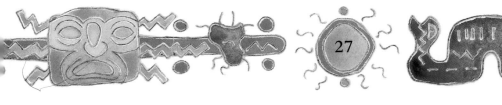

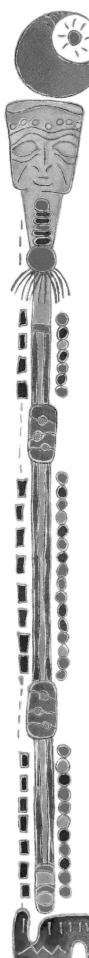

Some people—and there were plenty of people by now—were frightened by Maira-Monan.

"It's all very well for him to be creating all these different kinds of animals," commented one woman. "But what if he decides to turn his attentions to us? What if he decides that we should be a different shape?"

"Or color or size?" agreed her husband.

"What if he decides we should live in the oceans like fish? Who's to stop him?" demanded the woman. "He's too powerful."

"He must be stopped!" agreed their neighbor.

"Yes!" they chanted. "Yes!"

Finally a plan was hatched, and Maira-Monan was summoned to a nearby village.

"Thank you for coming, great page," said the village leader. Page is another name for shaman. "We have something to ask of you, but first we would like you to prove your powers we have heard so much about."

"If I must," said Maira-Monan, son of Irin-Mage. Unaware that this was a trap, the idea that he had to prove his power amused him. "What do you want me to do?"

"You must walk through a number of fires that we have prepared for you," said the villager leader.

"If that will satisfy you," said Maira-Monan, so they led him to the first fire.

He walked slowly through the flames—the bare soles of his feet treading on the burning embers as if they were nothing more than a few sharp pebbles—and came out the other side without so much as a smudge of ash on him.

"I don't know what that proves," said the great shaman, "but I am ready for your next fire."

So the villagers led him to the second fire. This fire contained magic that Maira-Monan was not expecting. No sooner had he stepped into the flames than he was overcome and stumbled to his knees. There were gasps from the onlookers. Had they really defeated him?

As the flames licked around Maira-Monan, he disappeared in an explosion of brilliant light followed by a noise so loud that it reached the heavens.

Those who had tricked him ran away in terror at what they had done, not knowing whether to shield their eyes or ears.

Up in the heavens the explosion reached a spirit called Tupan who caught the blinding flash and turned it into lightning and caught the rumbling "BOOM" and turned it into thunder. From that day forward Tupan became the spirit of thunder and lightning.

So every time there is a thunderstorm and lightning flashes, it is in memory of Maira-Monan. It also reminds us of the greatest storm the world has ever seen, when the creator flooded the earth and gave humans a second chance.

THE INCA—CHOSEN PEOPLE OF THE SUN

The fabulous Inca civilization, with its pyramid-shaped temples and wealth of gold, grew up in what is now Peru and then spread its empire up and down the Andes Mountains. This Inca myth tells where these people originally came from.

*P*acariqtambo, sometimes spelled *Paccari Tampu*, means "the place of origin" or "the dawn tavern." This was a place of three caves—three windows onto the world. Out of the middle cave stepped four brothers and four sisters, each dressed in the finest woolen shirts and blankets and each carrying beautiful vessels of the most intricately fashioned gold.

The brothers' names were Ayar Manco, Ayar Cachi, Ayar Auca, and Ayar Uchu. The four sisters were Mama Ocllo, Mama Raua, Mama Huaco, and Mama Cora. Out of the side caves came the people who were to be the ancestors of all the clans of the Inca people.

"These are the Inca, the chosen people of the Sun. They are our people," Ayar Manco told his brothers and sisters. "We must be their leaders and guide them to a land where they can live."

Ayar Manco carried a staff made of the finest gold. "We must test each place we visit with this staff," he said. "Where the staff sinks into the earth is the place where our people will settle."

The journey to find a homeland took several years, and over time the brothers and sisters grew tired of one member of their group.

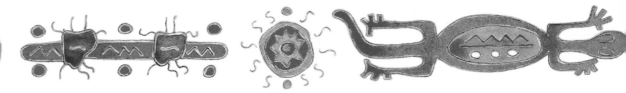

Ayar Cachi was always showing off his great strength and power, and one day he went too far.

They had climbed to the top of the mountain of Huanacauri and were looking at the land spread out before them.

"Somewhere down there is a place for our people to settle and build a mighty civilization," remarked Ayar Manco.

"It is a beautiful sight," said Mama Ocllo, the eldest of the sisters.

"But not beyond improvement," said Ayar Cachi, gathering up the loose stones at his feet.

Slipping the stones into a slingshot, he began firing them at the ground below . . . with such supernatural force that they made huge dents and furrows in the landscape, creating hills and ravines where the land was once flat.

"See. Even the earth itself bends to my will!" cried Ayar Cachi.

"He is becoming too powerful for his own good," said Mama Ocllo later that day.

"He must be stopped before he turns his strength against our people," said Ayar Manco. "We must protect the children of the Sun."

"He will not simply stop if we ask him," said Mama Raua. "How can we hope to silence him?"

"We will give him an important mission," said Ayar Manco, an idea forming in his mind. "One he cannot refuse. We will ask him to return to the great opening from which we came and to bring out the sacred llama to help us on our journey."

"And?" asked Ayar Auca.

"Once he is inside, we will wall him up inside the cave where he can do no more mischief!" said Ayar Manco.

"An excellent plan," agreed Mama Cora.

So Ayar Cachi's brothers and sisters went to him. "We have an important task, and you seem the obvious one to fulfill it," said Ayar Manco, and he asked his brother to return to the cave for the llama.

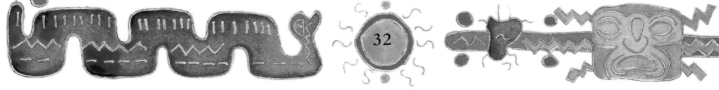

"Why should I go?" demanded Ayar Cachi.

"Because you are the fastest," said a sister.

"You are the fittest," said a brother.

"You tire less quickly," said another sister.

"It is true that I am quicker, fitter, and have greater stamina than you all," said Ayar Cachi. "I can see now why you want me to be the one to return to the cave for the sacred llama. I will go."

Just as Ayar Manco had predicted, his brother's pride had made him fall into their trap.

Unaware that he was being followed, Ayar Cachi returned to the caves at Pacariqtambo. No sooner had he stepped inside the middle cave from which all eight had originally entered this world than it was sealed up behind him.

"What's happening?" he cried, banging his huge fists against the wall of rock, but the rock remained solid, and his cries echoed in his ears.

"Let me out!" he demanded. "Let me out!"

Now there were only three brothers to continue the journey with their four sisters.

Ayar Uchu made an announcement: "I have decided to stay here at Huanacauri, from where our brother Ayar Cachi threw his stones."

His sisters begged him to go with them.

"Your duty lies with us and the Inca people," said Mama Raua.

"We need you," said Mama Huaco.

"Need me, Mama Huaco?" said Ayar Uchu. "I think not. You are a far greater fighter and warrior than I could ever be. You will do fine without me. My mind is made up."

"What will you do?" asked Mama Cora.

"I will watch over our people from this high place . . . forever," he said. And as these last words passed his lips, Ayar Uchu turned to stone.

Ayar Manco put his hands to the stone. "Goodbye, brother," he said, and turned away.

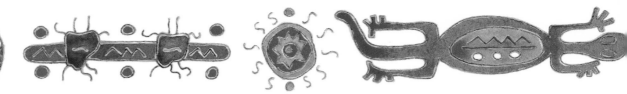

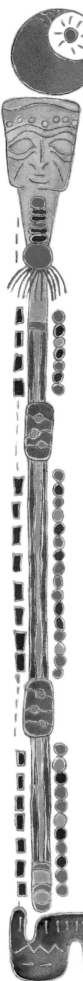

The chosen people built a shrine around the stone, and it became a sacred object.

Some say that Ayar Cachi somehow managed to escape from the cave at Pacariqtambo and that he joined Ayar Uchu on the mountaintop and that he, too, turned himself to stone. Whatever happened, only two of the four original brothers, Ayar Manco and Ayar Auca, continued their journey.

"I grow weary of traveling," Ayar Auca declared one morning. "Will we ever find a place for the Inca to settle?"

"We must and we will," said his sisters.

"But I travel better alone," said Ayar Auca.

With that he said goodbye to his brother Ayar Manco and to his sisters Mama Ocllo, Mama Raua, Mama Huaco, and Mama Cora and went his own way. Stories tell of how he eventually settled outside a city and, like his brothers before him, turned into a sacred stone.

This left Ayar Manco as the one remaining brother. It was he who went with his sisters to the valley of Cuzco. It was he who lowered the sacred golden staff to test the richness of the soil . . . and sank it right into the earth where it disappeared from view.

"Crops will grow well here," said Mama Ocllo. "This is a fertile place."

"This is the place where our people will settle and flourish," Ayar Manco announced.

"But other people already live here," Mama Cora reminded him.

"Then we must drive them away," said Mama Ocllo, who was now the mother of Ayar Manco's son, Sinchi Roca. "The Inca are the chosen people of the Sun. They need this land to grow their crops. Those already here must be made to give it up to them."

News of the arrival of the chosen people, led by Ayar Manco and his four sisters, soon spread. The people of the valley fought long and hard to defend their land, because their land was everything to them.

"They fight well," said Ayar Manco. "and they are many. How will we ever defeat them?"

"With fear," said Mama Huaco.

Ayar Uchu had been right. Mama Huaco was a great fighter and warrior. The next time the enemy attacked, she picked up her bola –stones tied together–and hurled it at her target. The bola wrapped around the man's head, killing him before he hit the ground.

As he lay in the dust, Mama Huaco cut out the man's lungs and blew into them so they swelled up like a bloated stomach. The people of the valley were so horrified by this sight that they turned and fled. Thanks to one of the four sisters from the middle cave of Pacariqtambo, the valley of Cuzco had been won for the Inca people.

After that Ayar Manco became known as Manco Capac, the founder of the Inca. It is said that he and his sisters built the first Inca homes in the valley with their own hands.

When the time came, Manco Capac turned to stone like his brothers before him. His son, Sinchi Roca, became the second emperor of the Inca–the chosen people of the Sun.

THE VOYAGE OF THE POPPYKETTLE

According to the Inca, El Niño ruled the wind, the weather, the ocean, and its creatures. El Niño was all-powerful and easily angered. This myth from Peru shows how El Niño could sometimes be kind, too.

Soon after the Spanish conquest, in a part of Peru that had been ruled by the mighty Inca before them, there lived gnomes as well as human beings . . . or so the story goes.

These gnomes wore clothes very similar to those of the Inca, who had ruled the empire, but they had long, shaggy hair and great big beards . . . great big beards for gnomes, that is. An Inca gnome's beard would barely cover the top of your thumb! And, like most gnomes the world over, these gnomes were always getting into mischief.

One day, in a place called Callo, which overlooked the sea, a small band of gnomes decided that enough was enough.

"We Inca gnomes enjoy fun," said one, "and fun is one thing we certainly don't have now that the Spaniards are our rulers. I say we should go somewhere else."

"A fine sentiment indeed," said a second gnome. "A fine sentiment. Where exactly should we go?"

"Why, there of course!" said a third, pointing to the horizon.

"What's there?" asked a fourth.

"Who knows?" said a fifth. "It would be exciting to find out."

"But how will we get there, wherever there is?" asked a sixth.

"Brown Pelican will help us," said the last member of the group of gnomes, which means–if you've been paying attention–that there must have been seven gnomes in this particular group.

Now Brown Pelican was a messenger to El Niño, lord of the weather, wind, and ocean. It was Brown Pelican's job to report to El Niño when people had been good and deserved his favor, and to report when they had been bad and deserved to be punished.

Brown Pelican liked the gnomes a lot more than he liked the Spanish invaders, but he didn't have time to fly them all the way to the horizon and beyond.

"But I will take you to Machu Picchu," said Brown Pelican.

"But why should we go there?" asked one of the gnomes.

Another one nudged him in the ribs. "Shh!" he hissed. "Or Brown Pelican might not want to take us anywhere."

"Good point," whispered a third, though he, too, wondered why the bird would want to take them to Machu Picchu–an Inca city, high in the Andes Mountains. Once this city had been full of life and color, but since the conquest it lay empty and in ruins.

"It's very kind of you to help us like this, but why Machu Picchu?" asked a fourth Inca gnome.

"You'll see," said Brown Pelican. "Climb onto my back, all of you, and hold on tight . . . but no tugging my feathers."

So the seven gnomes clambered up onto Brown Pelican's back. There was a bit of pushing and shoving as each tried to get the best view without being too near the edge. None of them wanted to fall off once they were up and away.

They landed in Machu Picchu on a ruined wall. "Here we are," said Brown Pelican. "I must be off now. Good luck with your voyage!"

"But why did you bring us here?" called out one of the bemused gnomes, still feeling rather blown about from the flight on Brown Pelican's back.

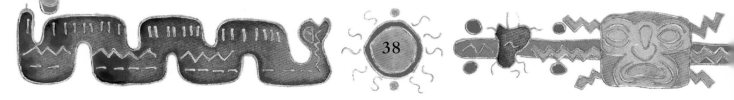

"To find you a ship," called out Brown Pelican, as he flew up into the sky. "You can't sail the seas without a ship."

"He's quite mad, you know," said one of the gnomes.

"Completely," agreed a second.

"He must be," agreed a third.

"How can we hope to find a ship up here?" asked a fourth.

"Look!" said a fifth.

"What?" asked a sixth.

"There!" said the seventh.

And they all crowded around an object resting on a nearby wall.

"It's a ship!" cried one with glee.

"Good old Brown Pelican!" cried another.

"Where are the sails?" asked a third.

"Good point!" said a fourth.

"We can make our own sails," said a fifth.

"Are you sure it's a ship?" asked a sixth.

"It's a gnome ship," said the seventh, "and a human poppykettle."

He was quite right. Made of clay, a poppykettle looks like a cross between an old-fashioned kettle and a teapot. It was used for brewing poppyseed tea. All you needed were poppyseeds, three brass keys–for flavor–and boiling water. But the seven Inca gnomes weren't about to brew up some tea. No. They set about turning the poppykettle into a ship!

When they were ready, El Niño sent them the great Silverado Bird on the wind. The gnomes had only just climbed aboard their ship–which they'd named the *Poppykettle*–when the bird swooped down, took the handle in its beak, and flew them down to the beach.

There more help was at hand, and a magical silver fish towed them out into the Pacific Ocean. Now their journey began in earnest.

A fair wind blew them toward the horizon, thanks to a little help from El Niño.

Then one day they came close to disaster. They found themselves sailing too close to the Iguana Islands where the dragon lizards lived.

"If we get much closer, the *Poppykettle* will be smashed against the rocky shore," cried one of the gnomes.

"If we get much closer, *we'll* be smashed on the shore," said another.

"If we get much closer, we'll be the dragons' lunch," said a third.

"What shall we do?" wailed a fourth.

"Blow on our sail," suggested a fifth.

"That's a silly idea!" said a sixth.

"Shut up and blow," said the seventh, and they all did.

But no matter how hard they tried to blow into the sail to make the ship leave the shore, the *Poppykettle* kept being blown inland.

As if things weren't bad enough, the tiny clay vessel caught the attention of one of the dragon lizards, which lumbered down to the rocks. Drooling at the thought of seven whole gnomes for lunch, the creature's jaw dropped and—as happens with most dragons—flames and hot air spurted out.

Fortunately for our band of travelers, the flames didn't reach them, but the hot air did. It filled their sails and blew the ship away from the shore, back out to sea. There was a lot of cheering as the *Poppykettle* was caught in a current and sailed on to safety.

The seven Inca gnomes had many more adventures in their poppykettle craft. . . . One time they were caught in a terrible storm. Day after day huge waves crashed against the *Poppykettle*, tossing it up into the air and crashing it down on the ocean . . . until the storm finally subsided.

"Phew," said one.

"That was a close call," said a second.

"I thought we were going to drown," said a third.

"There's a crack in the *Poppykettle*," said a fourth.

"There's water coming in!" added a fifth.

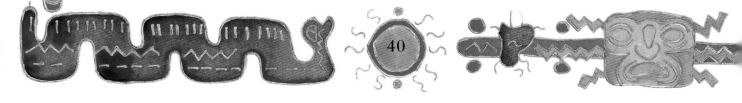

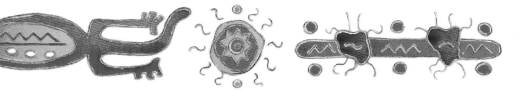

"Abandon ship!" cried the sixth.

"None of us can swim!" pointed out the seventh.

"Don't panic!" said a passing dolphin, tossing the *Poppykettle* —with the seven gnomes inside it—onto his back.

"We're being kidnapped!" yelped all the little gnomes at once.

"No, you're not," said the dolphin (and don't forget that El Niño ruled over all the creatures in the oceans). "I'm giving you a free ride."

The gnomes were grateful. They really were. But dolphins have a habit of jumping out of the water in graceful arches, just for the fun of it, and whenever that happened, the *Poppykettle*—with them inside it—went tumbling down the dolphin's back.

In the end they solved this problem by lashing their vessel around the dolphin's neck—or rather where a dolphin's neck would be if it had one—until they reached dry land.

"We've arrived!" shouted the gnomes, tumbling onto the sand with glee. "We've arrived!" But they had no idea where they were.

In fact, so the myth goes, El Niño's wind, waves, and sea creatures had carried the seven Inca gnomes all the way to Australia, where they lived out their days having fun!

ASARE AND THE ALLIGATORS

An old Sherente myth tells of a group of seven brothers who disgraced their parents and so had to leave the safety of their village. The youngest of the brothers was Asare, and he had many adventures. This is just one of them.

"Come on, try to keep up!" said the eldest. "We've a long way to go, Asare."

"But I'm thirsty," protested the boy. They had been walking for many hours now, and his throat was dry.

"That's simple enough to solve," said the eldest. "Look." He pointed to a cluster of tucum nuts up a tree, which, like coconuts, contain a sweet liquid.

The brothers hurried to find a stick long enough to knock the nuts to the ground. They scurried here and there, and it was Asare who finally found a broken branch in the undergrowth.

"Here," he said, excitedly. He put down his hunting arrow and handed the broken piece of branch to his eldest brother.

His brother used the branch to knock the tucum nuts from the tree with a loud "THWACK," followed by another "THWACK" as they hit the ground.

The brothers hurried forward and split open the nuts to give their youngest brother a drink.

Asare drank the water from nut after nut after nut. But he was still so thirsty that they had to find another tree and knock down another cluster of nuts . . . and still his thirst wasn't quenched.

"You can't still be thirsty!" protested one of his brothers, angrily.

"But I am," cried Asare, upset that he was being shouted at.

"Don't worry," said the eldest. "There should be water just below the surface of the ground down in that hollow. We'll dig a well."

Everyone was excited by this idea. One good thing about having left the village was that there were no elders telling them what to do.

So the brothers walked down into the hollow and began to dig, first with their hands and later with sticks. Eventually there was a mighty "WHOOOOOSH!" and water began spurting out of the ground.

Asare drank until he was fit to burst, and still the water poured from the ground. It formed the first river . . . which later grew into a lake and then turned into the oceans.

In the beginning, the brothers were stunned by the sight of the river. Then the eldest grinned, realizing its advantages.

"Now whenever you're thirsty, all you need to do is take a drink from those waters," he said.

But Asare wasn't smiling. "I left my arrow on the spot where I found the branch to knock down the tucum nuts," he groaned. "And that's on the other side of the water."

"Then you'll have to make yourself a new arrow," snapped another of his six brothers.

"No," said Asare. "That arrow has brought me luck when hunting."

"That's true enough," agreed the eldest. "Think of all the lizards you killed with it along the way."

Asare groaned a second time. The lizards would have been washed away by the water when the river was formed.

"The lizards may be lost," he said, which meant one less meal for the traveling brothers, "but at least I can rescue my arrow."

Before the others had time to protest, he'd jumped into the water and was making his way across to the other side. None of his brothers dared to follow him.

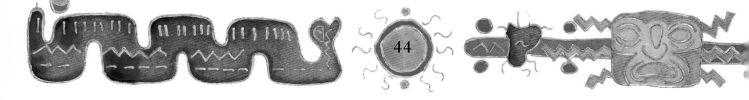

"It's too dangerous," said one.

"He could kill himself," said another.

But Asare was already scrambling up the opposite bank and scurrying back to where he'd put his favorite arrow, which, fortunately, was still on dry land.

Asare found it harder coming back the other way. For a start, he was clutching the arrow in one hand, and second, the more water that gushed from the hole he and his brothers had dug, the stronger the river's current became.

Asare made a desperate grab for a floating log that was bobbing by and released his grasp on the arrow in the process . . . only it wasn't a passing log at all–it was an alligator.

Now Asare can't be blamed for making this mistake. He had never seen an alligator before, because there had never been any alligators before–in the same way that there had been no rivers or oceans until now.

This was one of the very first alligators on earth. In fact, before the brothers had dug the hole, this alligator had been one of the lizards Asare had caught. But once it had been swept away in the water, it turned into an alligator. It did look very much like a log, except that it had mean eyes and row upon row of very sharp teeth.

"Let go of me!" demanded the alligator.

Asare did as he was told but found it hard to keep his head above water. "Let me sit on your back, Mister ugly nose," he said, "and give me a ride to the other side."

"No," said the alligator and began snapping its jaws.

This frightened Asare enough to give him a new burst of energy, and he found himself swimming through the strong current to reach the other side.

There was no sign of his brothers anywhere. They had seen Asare's arrow floating down the river and assumed that he had drowned.

Although he was on dry land once more, Asare soon discovered that his troubles weren't over. Unlike logs, not only did alligators have mean eyes and teeth but they also had legs . . . and this particular alligator was using those legs to follow Asare into the forest.

"I may have an ugly nose, but it's a big one and it will sniff you out, little human!" the alligator called out, not far behind him.

Up ahead Asare heard the "TAP-TAP" of woodpeckers pecking the bark off a tree. Asare begged for their help, and the woodpeckers covered the boy from head to toe with pieces of bark.

This not only made Asare look like a scaly monster–a bit like an upright alligator–but the bark of the tree also disguised his smell.

When the angry alligator came crashing through the undergrowth, it didn't recognize him at all. "Has a human come this way?" it asked.

"He went that way," said Asare, pointing deep into the forest, and the woodpeckers nodded their heads in agreement.

With a grunt the alligator headed off on the false trail.

Asare thanked the woodpeckers, threw off his disguise, and made his way back to the river. He'd only been in the water a few moments when he came face to face with another alligator. He didn't even consider asking this one to carry him across the river. He tried to swim around it, but it gave chase.

Again Asare found himself heading for the forest and thought he could hear voices up ahead. Was this the sound of his brothers? Had they crossed the river to rescue him? Was he safe at last? His brothers had arrows and could frighten the alligator. But no–it was a group of monkeys, busy eating fruit and chattering about the day's events.

"Please hide me," said the boy. "I'm being chased by a creature from the river, and it has plenty of teeth."

When the monkeys saw Asare, they grew quiet and stared.

One of them pointed to the skins of the jatoba fruit they were eating, which were heaped in a big pile in front of them.

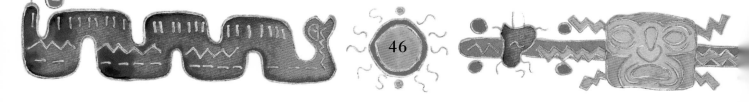

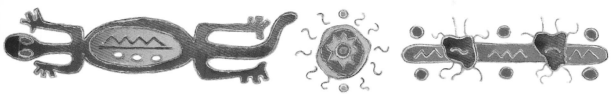

Asare had barely had time to wriggle under the pile and hide when the second alligator appeared in the clearing.

"Have you seen a boy?" it asked.

"You're a funny-looking creature," said one of the monkeys, who couldn't help commenting on the alligator's appearance.

"I've seen lots of boys," said another.

"In fact—" began the third monkey, about to tell the alligator about Asare hiding under the jatoba skins, because most monkeys are terrible at keeping secrets. They just can't help it.

Fortunately for Asare another monkey hit the talkative monkey on the lips before it could give the game away, and the alligator made off into the undergrowth.

Thanking the monkeys, Asare came out from his hiding place and swam across the river. At long last he caught up with his brothers, who were amazed and delighted that he was still alive.

Together they bathed in the newly formed ocean. They became so clean and shiny that they now gleam in the sky as seven stars, called the Seven Brothers.

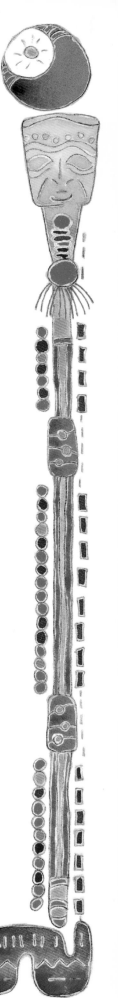

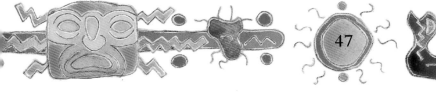

INDEX

African Americans 4
Andes, a mountain range 4, 31, 38
Argentina 4
Asare 43-47

Bolivia 4
Bororo myth 7-11
Bororo people 3, 7
Botoque, the first human to eat
   cooked meat 13-17
Brazil 2
Brown Pelican, messenger to
   El Niño 38-39

Carajá myth 19-23
Carajá people 3, 19
Chile 2, 4
climate 2
Colombia 2
Cuzco, first Inca home 34, 35

Ecuador 4
El Dorado, the Golden Man 5
El Niño, ruler of the wind, weather,
   and oceans 37, 38, 39, 41
Europeans 2, 4

fire, the secret of 13, 15-17, 25-29

gnomes 37-41
gold 4, 5, 31
grasslands 3, 19

Huanacauri, a mountain 32, 33

Iguana Islands, home of the dragon
   lizards 40
Inca myths 31-35, 37-41
Inca people 3, 4-5, 31-35, 37, 38
Irin-Mage, father of humankind
   26-27

jaguar 13, 15-17
James I, King of England 5
jatoba, a tree 15, 46-47

Kaboi, a very wise man 19-23
Kayapó myth 13-17
Kayapó people 3, 13

macaw, a clever bird 7-10, 13-15
Machu Picchu, an ancient Inca
   city 38
Maira-Monan, son of Irin-Mage
   27-29
Manco Capac, founder of the Inca
   35
Monan, Tupinambá creator god
   25-27

Pacariqtambo, the place of origin
   31, 33, 35
Peru 2, 4, 31, 37
Poppykettle, a sailing vessel 37,
   39-41

Raleigh, Sir Walter, an English
   explorer 5
religion 2, 25

savanna 19, 20
seriema, a bird 19, 20, 21, 23
shamans 27, 28
Sherente myth 43-47
Sherente people 3, 43
Sinchi Roca, second emperor
   of the Inca 34, 35
South America, the continent 2-3
South American peoples 2-3, 4, 5
   see also under individual groups
Spanish conquest 5, 37, 38
stars, the creation of 7-11
sun gods 5

Tata, a terrible fire from heaven 26
trickster animals 4
Tupan, the spirit of thunder and
   lightning 29
Tupinambá myth 25-29
Tupinambá people 3, 25

First published in the UK in 1998 by

Belitha Press Ltd
   London House, Great Eastern Wharf
   Parkgate Road, London SW11 4NQ

Copyright in this format
© Belitha Press 1998
Text copyright © Philip Ardagh 1998
Illustrations copyright © Belitha Press 199[8]

Philip Ardagh asserts his moral right to
be identified as the author of this work.

Editor: Julie Hill
Designer: Jamie Asher
Educational consultant: Liz Bassant
Series editor: Mary-Jane Wilkins

Printed in Hong Kong

Published in the United States in 1999 by
Dillon Press
An Imprint of Macmillan Library
   Reference USA
A Division of Prentice-Hall, Inc.
1633 Broadway, New York, NY 10019

Library of Congress
Cataloging-in-Publication Data

Ardagh, Philip.
   South American myths & legends / Phil[ip]
Ardagh.
      p.   cm.
   Originally published: London, England:
Belitha Press, 1998.
   Includes index.
   Summary: Retells some traditional storie[s]
from various native peoples of South Ame[rica]
including the Kayapo, Sherente, Caraja, Bo[roro]
and Tupinamba.
   1. Indian mythology--South America.
2. Tales--South America. 3. Legends--Sou[th]
America. [1. Indians of South America--
Folklore. 2. Folklore--South America.] I[.]
F2230.1.R3A73   1998
[398.2'08998]--dc21   98-
ISBN 0-382-42004-7 (LSB)
10 9 8 7 6 5 4 3 2 1